BEYOND THE STEPS:
MULTICULTURAL STUDY GUIDE

Festus E. Obiakor, Ph.D.
Emporia State University

KENDALL/HUNT PUBLISHING COMPANY
4050 Westmark Drive   Dubuque, Iowa 52002

Copyright © 1999 by Festus E. Obiakor

ISBN 0-7872-5717-6

Printed in the United States of America
10 9 8 7 6 5 4

CONTENTS

PREFACE

Beyond the Steps: Multicultural Study Guide is written with the simple intention of making the original text, *The Eight-Step Multicultural Approach: Learning and Teaching with a Smile* more user-friendly. I believe education must have the power to change; and for this power to be less dramatic, it must be related to practice. Multicultural education must be viewed as the hub that connects all educational practices. It must never be viewed as an emotional or exotic phenomenon -- it must be studied, learned, and instructed (Obiakor, 1994). Additionally, it must be viewed as a *powerful* force that complements other theories of learning like humanism, behaviorism, and cognitive learning theory (Pederson, 1991).

Our classrooms, schools, and communities are changing demographically. Individuals who look, talk, behave, and learn differently are no longer invisible. The traditional Eurocentric process has tried to forcibly assimilate these individuals (Banks, 1999; Grossman, 1998a,1998b). Ironically, any form of assimilation consumes the personal identities that ultimately solidify the sacred existence of these individuals. Individual differences must be valued, learned, and infused in all educational processes (e.g., identification, assessment, categorization, placement, and instruction)(Baca & Cervantes, 1991; Ford, Obiakor, & Patton, 1995; Winzer & Mazurek, 1998). The society loses when individuals are misidentified, misassessed, miscategorized, misplaced, and misinstructed. For education to be practical, the society must avoid prejudicial expectations, biased generalizations, and illusory conclusions. In a nutshell, classrooms, schools, and communities must increase the quality of life of those that come in contact with them. They must be environments where (a) individuals' self-concepts are enhanced, (b) personal values are highlighted, (c) crises are managed, and (d) community members collaborate, consult, and cooperate (Obiakor & Algozzine, 1995; Obiakor, Mehring, & Schwenn, 1997).

Beyond the Steps is aimed at improving the learning-teaching process. To facilitate this process, each *step* has:

1. *Learning-Teaching Objectives* — these objectives present strategic highlights for *learners*. From my perspective, the "learner" includes the student, teacher, or any professional. We are involved in the learning-teaching process as we interact with people different from us. I believe education should be a continuous process of growth in our multicultural classrooms, schools, and communities.

2. *Discussion and Study Activities* — these activities expose learning-teaching imperatives. In some fashion, these activities are central to ideas that must be mastered by *learners*.

3. *Examination Questions* — these questions provide pertinent avenues for *learners* to apply, analyze, synthesize, and evaluate the knowledge they have gained and comprehended.

Beyond the Steps is a helpful guide to experienced and new learners; however, teachers, parents, administrators, and community leaders will find it very useful. Though this multicultural study guide is arranged to conform with the steps in *The Eight-Step Multicultural Approach*, it has a mind of its own. It provides learners with new ideas, new thinking, and new techniques for responding to racial, cultural, linguistic, and socio-economic differences. The steps might be hierarchical, but the ideas are not. Ideas are presented to stimulate critical thinking and to foster harmonious relationships in any organization. Some ideas are even repeated to emphasize continuity. Such a continuity is necessary because it foreshadows continuous cultural enhancement and community interaction. Our society is well-served when cultural continuity responds to and interacts with our changing times.

Beyond the Steps would have been an impossibility without the integrated support of my family, friends, and well-wishers. I strongly believe projects of this nature cannot materialize without a *Comprehensive Support Model* (CSM) which incorporates the "self," family, schools, and communities (Obiakor, 1994). For instance, my wife, Pauline and our children, Charles, Gina, and Kristen provided lots of love and support. Under the direction of Deborah Mulsow of the Teachers College Word Processing Department, Emporia State University, Emporia, Kansas, the initial manuscript was typed and organized. And finally, my friends and well-wishers provided wonderful experiences that engineered the writing of this multicultural study guide. I left my comfort zone when I immigrated from Nigeria to the United States many years ago. I am convinced more than before that I would not have traveled successfully to my current destination without the dedicated support of many people from different racial, cultural, linguistic, and socio-economic backgrounds. I hope that using this multicultural study guide will provide the reader with important directions as he/she travels in this journey of life.

STEP ONE

KNOW WHO YOU ARE

Step One, Know Who You Are, presents the springboard for the learning-teaching process. It is difficult for us to work with people different from us if we do not know our strengths, weaknesses, and personal idiosyncracies (Obiakor, 1994). Our knowledge of who we are is not easy; and who we are reflects our deeper meaning and our projected actions. These actions must be *real* and divorced from gimmicks. Who we say we are might be different from who we really are. When this happens, we create confusions that lend themselves to strange interpretations of our very being. These interpretations can have far-reaching effects on our self-identity, self-valuation, and self-empowerment (Obiakor & Algozzine, 1994; Obiakor, Algozzine, & Campbell-Whatley, 1997).

Our histories, our values, and our cultures must help us to frame who we are. We cannot deny them, and we cannot downplay them. Our attempts to do these can lead to racial and cultural devaluing, and to a larger extent, our personal devaluing. For us to know who we are, we must engage in a painstaking evaluation of our interactions with ourselves and others (Obiakor, Campbell-Whatley, Schwenn, & Dooley, 1998). We must value these interactions and see how they intermingle with our body, mind, and soul. Our knowledge of who we are must produce a balance that could help us to interpret our reality, beauty, knowledge, and truth (see Obiakor et al., 1998).

LEARNING-TEACHING OBJECTIVES

After reading Step One, the learner will be able to:
1. Examine his/her beliefs and explain how these beliefs are influenced by cultural values, racial backgrounds, linguistic differences, and socio-economic backgrounds.
2. Explore his/her attitudes toward other people who look, talk, behave, and learn differently.
3. Listen actively to himself/herself and to others.
4. Analyze reasons for his/her sacred existence (i.e., being).
5. Evaluate reasons for choosing to do what he/she does (e.g., student, educator, psychologist, therapist, and clinician).

DISCUSSION AND STUDY ACTIVITIES

Discussion and study activities for Step One include, but are not limited to the following:
1. Take an attitude survey to see how you feel about various issues.
2. Talk with other people to see how they feel and think about issues dear to your heart or dear to their hearts.
3. Discover who you are by researching your origin (e.g., family tree).
4. Write down reasons for your being (e.g., reasons for being a student, teacher, or a member of your chosen profession).

5. Learn the views of others by listening actively to them.
6. Demonstrate reasons for your similarities and dissimilarities with others.
7. Describe your strengths, weaknesses, and personal idiosyncracies.
8. Ask yourself questions related to your self-knowledge, self-love, and self-empowerment.
9. Create opportunities for you to tell your stories -- your stories might be similar or dissimilar from others.
10. Examine how you are connected to your school, community, state, nation, and world.

Name: **Date:**

EXAMINATION

Following are examination questions based on objectives and pertinent ideas of Step One of *The Eight-Step Multicultural Approach*:

1. Identify *two* things you like about yourself and *two* things you dislike about yourself. Explain reasons for your decision.

7

2. Briefly describe who you are. In your description, include your culture, race, language, socio-economic background, and national origin.

3.   **Explain how your beliefs and values affect your relationship with people different from you.**

4. Some scholars and educators have indicated that we are all prejudiced. Do you agree? Give reasons for your answer.

5. Briefly analyze how your knowledge of who you are can affect your ability to excel or not excel in your chosen profession.

STEP TWO

WHEN IN DOUBT, LEARN THE FACTS

Step Two, When in Doubt, Learn the Facts, suggests that our knowledge of events is not genetically handed-down and that for growth to be possible, we must learn the facts. When we learn the facts, we avoid prejudicial expectations, biased judgments, racist generalizations, and illusory conclusions (Obiakor, 1994). We must learn that culture is a complex web which unites beliefs, arts, morals, laws, customs, capabilities, and habits acquired by an individual in a particular society. We must also learn that multicultural education enhances the *full* scope of education -- multicultural education is not another welfare program that denigrates the quality of education. It is a cost-effective way to tap the human resources of *all* Americans (Banks, 1999). By so doing, it exposes individuals to maximum knowledge and learning.

I believe education must have the tendency to change attitudes -- education must be different from training or indoctrination. A teacher must be a learner, collaborator, consultant, and team player -- he/she must also be someone who involves, includes, and empowers (Dettmer, Dyck, & Thurston, 1996). General and special educators must learn to be great critical thinkers, creative planners, and effective practitioners. Quality results can never be achieved in the learning-teaching process unless educators learn to incorporate other cultures in their identification, assessment, and instruction of students.

LEARNING-TEACHING OBJECTIVES

After reading Step Two, the learner will be able to:
1. Explain what multicultural education means to him/her.
2. Examine the relationship between multicultural education and quality education.
3. Analyze the dangers of excluding multicultural issues in educational or psychological programming.
4. Evaluate the role of the teacher or related professional in the context of multicultural education.
5. Describe, in historical contexts, his/her past and present knowledge of multicultural education.

DISCUSSION AND STUDY ACTIVITIES

Discussion and study activities for Step Two include, but are not limited to the following:
1. Take a course about a culture different from your own.
2. Attend a multicultural celebration and event taking place in your community.
3. Talk with parents, students, and fellow colleagues, and have each person share his/her own family traditions and customs.
4. Recount your travel experiences (e.g., what it means to be different at a new location.)
5. Discover information on other cultures and demonstrate appreciation for individual differences.

6. Research alternative views on popular notions in psychology and education.
7. Allow learners or participants to instruct on topics related to their cultural backgrounds.
8. Accommodate individual needs during discussions.
9. Discourage any sign of *invisibility* and encourage shared ownership.
10. Practice "show and tell" as many times as possible to incorporate family and community activities.

Name: **Date:**

EXAMINATION

Following are examination questions based on objectives and pertinent ideas of Step Two of *The Eight-Step Multicultural Approach*:

    1.   **Based on information in Step Two, in your own words, define multicultural education.**

2. Briefly describe how your knowledge of multicultural education has influenced your relationship with people around you.

3. One's thinking can change by what he/she has learned about others. Do you agree? Give reasons for your answer.

4. Briefly explain *two* issues you have learned from reading Step Two. You must also explain what these issues mean to you as a human being.

5. Evaluate the role of a teacher or professional in learning-teaching contexts of multicultural education.

STEP THREE

CHANGE YOUR THINKING

Step Three, Change Your Thinking, indicates that the knowledge we have gained is a vain glory unless it results in a change of how we think. When our thinking is static, we become inflexible to new ideas and slaves to old unworkable ideas (Obiakor, 1994). Having the knowledge and ability to comprehend it is not enough. We must be willing to apply it, analyze it, synthesize it, and evaluate it. By so doing, our thinking paradigms are stimulated to shift. What makes our environment "good" or "bad" sometimes depends on our thinking of what is "good" or "bad." Our traditional definitions appear to be static because they fail to respond to perceptions of environmental stimuli that frequently result in the formation of cognitive structures. Thinking results in new ideas and new ways of problem-solving. Our traditional thinking about race, ethnicity, and prejudice will only change when we challenge them (Banks, 1999; Gollnick & Chinn, 1998; West, 1993).

Many retrogressive views still exist because we refuse to think about ways to modify them to address current demographic trends. For instance, many people still assume that all African American children are "poor" and that since they are "poor," they have "poor" intelligence and "poor" self-concepts. These traditional views consistently lead to misidentification, misassessment, miscategorization, misplacement, and misinstruction (Baca & Cervantes, 1991; Ford, Obiakor, & Patton, 1995). In reality, many African American children have high resiliency and creativity levels that manifest themselves in classroom, school, and community activities. On the other hand, it is erroneous to assume that all White people discriminate against minorities. In reality, many Whites have supported non-Whites on issues related to racial prejudice and discrimination (see Obiakor, 1994). It is important that we change our thinking on how issues are viewed traditionally. Our paradigms can never be shifted unless our thinking is changed.

LEARNING-TEACHING OBJECTIVES

After reading Step Three, the learner will be able to:
1. Discuss what "change" means to him/her.
2. Explain how his/her ideas about multicultural education have changed since taking this course.
3. Describe how his/her interaction with someone from a different cultural or linguistic background has changed his/her thinking.
4. Demonstrate knowledge about the advantages of thinking in problem-solving.
5. Evaluate why thinking is inevitable in human relations.

DISCUSSION AND STUDY ACTIVITIES

Discussion and study activities for Step Three include, but are not limited to the following:
1. Expose your peers/colleagues to historical values of your culture.
2. Allow your peers/colleagues to share historical values of their cultures.
3. Question your thinking, performance, and motivation.

4. Respect and celebrate the uniqueness of every learner in your class/group.
5. Open your mind and believe in yourself and others around you.
6. Develop friendships in your class/group.
7. Discuss with others what makes you comfortable or uncomfortable.
8. Describe how you can get out of your comfort zone.
9. Explain what change means to you, and learn what it means to other people.
10. Discuss how your thinking has changed based on what you have learned from others.

Name: **Date:**

EXAMINATION

Following are examination questions based on objectives and pertinent ideas of Step Three of *The Eight-Step Multicultural Approach*:

1. "Changing perceptions about people, events, and situations is painstaking. We all have to be willing to leave our comfort zones." In your own words, briefly explain this statement.

2. Discuss what the term, "change" means to you. Use examples to answer this question.

3. **Evaluate why thinking is a necessity in cultural and human relations.**

4. Briefly discuss how your thinking about multicultural education has changed.

5. Explain reasons for change in your chosen profession. Use examples to answer this question.

STEP FOUR

USE RESOURCE PERSONS

Step Four, Use Resource Persons, recognizes all human-beings (Whites and non-Whites) as useful and capable resources (Obiakor, 1994). In my Multicultural Psychology and Special Education course, I frequently pose the question, "Who are resource persons?" This question has consistently created difficulties for my undergraduate and graduate students whenever asked. Recently, however, one of my undergraduate students responded: "We are all resource persons." The student's answer was correct because it correlates with the popular African statement: "It takes a whole village to raise a child." This statement is also sensible because it creates a mutually inclusive environment that recognizes all individuals as contributors to our daily survival. Students, teachers, service providers, parents, guardians, business people, and other members of the community are resource persons. We cannot ignore them or downplay them (Obiakor, 1994). When we ignore them, we ignore very important parts of our positive or negative connections.

We must recognize various school, family, and community entities -- these entities will intervene in crises and provide necessary information and services when needed (Obiakor, Mehring, & Schwenn, 1997). In other words, students, parents, teachers, and community members must support each other in all matters. Any lack of support reveals negativism which can lead to misinformation, gross generalizations, and illusory conclusions. When individuals work with each other, they tend to understand each other's problems. Such an understanding can foster collaboration, consultation, and cooperation -- common concerns lead to common solutions (Dettmer, Dyck, & Thurston, 1996). Our society is well-served when we use each other's strengths and when we work on each other's problems. Our current educational and societal problems (e.g., misidentification, misassessment, miscategorization, and misinstruction) cannot be solved unless we value and empower ourselves as resource persons. No one person can solve all our human problems. The only way is for us to tap our human resources and talents (see Dettmer et al., 1996).

LEARNING - TEACHING OBJECTIVES

After reading Step Four, the learner will be able to:
1.   Explain who resource persons are.
2.   Describe how the use of resource persons relates to multicultural education.
3.   Examine how the use of resource persons can improve educational programming.
4.   Summarize the relationship between collaboration and consultation in general and special education.
5.   Analyze reasons for positive partnerships between parents and professionals.

DISCUSSION AND STUDY ACTIVITIES

Discussion and study activities for Step Four include, but are not limited to the following:
1.   When studying another culture, invite a guest speaker from that culture to speak to your class/group.

2. Ask parents to come to your classroom and talk about their culture.
3. Team with another person in your school/program to improve collaboration.
4. Invite an exchange student who has come to your community to talk to your class/group.
5. Initiate contact with a neighboring school or college.
6. Create an open door atmosphere that fosters honest questions and answers.
7. Begin each year by sending letters home to parents and guardians to provide personal information.
8. Share information concerning programs with parents/guardians in an empowering way.
9. Encourage students or program participants to work with each other.
10. Allow parents or guardians to visit and teach classes.

Name: **Date:**

EXAMINATION

       Following are examination questions based on objectives and pertinent ideas of Step Four of *The Eight-Step Multicultural Approach*:

       1.   **In your own words, explain who resource persons are.**

2.   Examine how the use of resource persons can improve the quality of education.

Kevin

3. **Briefly explain the relationship between collaboration and consultation in educational programming.**

Collab: working with parents to enhance the educational, social and life - experience of the student.

Consultation: To give advice based on one's experience, background and academic upbringing. Usually from expert to Novice.

4. **Analyze reasons for positive relationships between parents and professionals.**

A positive experience/relationship with parents provides a solid foundation in which the student can grow from or be built up from. It gives the student direction and it gives the educator the parental support needed to help the student grow.

5. "Resource persons are very useful." Do you agree. Use examples to support your answer.

STEP FIVE

BUILD SELF-CONCEPTS

Step Five, Build Self-Concepts, discusses one of the fundamental aims of education (i.e., how to build self-concepts of learners) (Obiakor, 1994). Traditionally, self-concept is viewed as an interrelated perception of the self. This viewpoint is based on perception; and perception is based on an unscientific judgment or gut feeling. Gut feelings result in misconception, misidentification, mislabeling, and misinstruction. They also lead to biased representations and illusory conclusions. Contemporarily, self-concept is viewed as an individual's repertoire of self-descriptive behaviors. It is operational, multidimensional, accurate, inaccurate, functional, situation-specific, area-specific, and liable to change as contexts change (Obiakor, Algozzine, & Campbell-Whatley, 1997; Obiakor & Stile, 1994). This viewpoint seems to regard self-concept as a construct that is explainable, describable, measurable, quantifiable, and observable, In this case, gut feelings have little or no involvement.

To enhance self-concepts of multicultural learners who are frequently at-risk of misperception, general and special educators must understand the meaning of self-concept. Let's assume that one knows who he/she is (i.e., self-knowledge), it does not necessarily mean that he/she must love himself/herself (i.e., self-esteem). Additionally, an individual might love himself/herself and not demonstrate willingness to expend effort to achieve his/her goals (i.e., self-ideal). Though self-understanding, self-love, and self-empowerment are intricate variables of self-concept, they differ in constructs and meanings (Obiakor & Stile, 1994), and their implications to multicultural learners are multidimensional (Obiakor & Algozzine, 1994). One, the unique needs of multicultural learners will be addressed. Two, it will be easy to design specific programs (e.g., Individualized Education Plans) for multicultural learners. Three, multicultural learners will not be judged on the basis of gut feeling. And fourth, self-concept of multicultural learners will not be viewed as genetic phenomenon that cannot be enhanced. As a consequence, general and special educators must (a) have realistic expectations, (b) avoid unnecessary labels, (c) reduce prejudicial generalizations, (d) stop illusory conclusions, and (e) create rewarding environments (Obiakor & Algozzine, 1994, 1995; Obiakor & Schwenn, 1995).

LEARNING - TEACHING OBJECTIVES

After reading Step Five, the learner will be able to:
1. Differentiate between the traditional and contemporary definitions of self-concept.
2. Explain the multidimentionality of self-concepts.
3. Summarize the benefits of looking at self-concept as an operational construct.
4. Describe the dangers of misperception.
5. Explain ways to enhance self-concepts of multicultural learners.

DISCUSSION AND STUDY ACTIVITIES

Discussion and study activities for Step Five include, but are not limited to the following:
1. Have a "nice-words" policy at the beginning of the program.

2. Use a balanced information about cultures as you teach.
3. Utilize cooperative learning techniques to expose individual strengths of students.
4. Have realistic expectations about learners.
5. Believe that everyday is a new day.
6. Provide students with opportunities to meet new challenges.
7. Challenge each child to be the best.
8. Reflect upon the day's events.
9. Allow students or participants to find answers to open-ended questions.
10. Avoid labels in your program.

EXAMINATION

Following are examination questions based on objectives and pertinent ideas of Step Five of *The Eight-Step Multicultural Approach*:

1.   In your own words, define self-concept operationally.

2.   **Differentiate between the traditional and contemporary definitions of self-concept.**

3. Self-concept is multidimensional. Evaluate this statement. Use examples to answer this question.

4.   Self-concept is not genetically handed-down -- it can certainly be enhanced. Do you agree? Briefly explain how self-concept can be enhanced for multicultural learners.

5. Describe the dangers of prejudicial expectations on multicultural learners. Use examples to answer this question.

STEP SIX

TEACH WITH DIVERGENT TECHNIQUES

Step Six, Teach with Divergent Techniques, focuses on the multidimensionality of teaching methods that respond to individual differences in students' learning styles, cultural backgrounds, and multiple intelligences (Gardner, 1993; Obiakor, 1994). General and special educators are traditionally prepared to address the unique needs of students in classrooms, schools, and communities. The undergirding principle is to recognize that students differ inter-individually and intra-individually. Based on this principle, students and their parents are valued as individuals from different racial, linguistic, cultural, and socio-economic backgrounds. In spite of this fundamental principle, general and special educators continue to be tied to the apron string of one technique based on a Eurocentric culture (Banks, 1999; Grossman, 1998a, 1998b; Obiakor, 1997). In many cases, students' linguistic and socio-economic backgrounds are ignored or downplayed. As a consequence, students who look, talk, behave, and learn differently in classroom, school, and community programs are misidentified, misassessed, misplaced, mislabeled, and misinstructed (Gould, 1981). These students continue to bear the brunt of most educational shortcomings (Obiakor & Utley, 1997).

The intriguing question is, If we assume that we understand the fundamentals of individual indifferences, why do we impose on students one technique based on one theory or model (e.g., psychodynamic model, biophysical model, environmental model, humanistic model, behavioral model, and cognitive learning model)? Our understanding of any educational concept is meaningless unless we apply, analyze, synthesize, and evaluate it. Imperatively, general and special educators must (a) be knowledgeable about and sensitive to students' cultural and linguistic backgrounds, (b) demonstrate respect for cultures different from their own, (c) provide an atmosphere in which cultures are valued, (d) use and supplement culturally appropriate curricular materials as needed, (e) give learners the opportunity to teach, (f) eradicate stereotypes that impinge upon learning behaviors, and (g) involve parents and community members in classroom and school activities (Obiakor, 1994). In more specific terms, the direct needs of multicultural learners will be addressed when classroom teachers (a) vary their stimuli, (b) use greater verbal interaction, (d) stimulate divergent thinking, (e) incorporate the use of dialects, (f) present real-world tasks, (g) include a people focus, (h) infuse cooperative learning, (i) encourage group activities, and (j) incorporate peer tutorial (Obiakor, 1994). In more general terms, educators will help *all* learners maximize their fullest potential when they (a) develop real pedagogical power, (b) avoid the poverty of the teaching spirit, (c) desist from the band-aid teaching phenomenon, (d) stop iatrogenic teaching methods of solving problems that do not exist, and (e) develop an espirit de corps and a sense of decorum in teaching (Banks, 1999; Hilliard, 1995; Winzer & Mazurek, 1998).

LEARNING-TEACHING OBJECTIVES

After reading Step Six, the learner will be able to:
1.   Explain the phrase, "teach with divergent techniques."
2.   Examine the undergirding principle in learning and teaching.

3. Analyze the concept of individual differences.
4. Describe how students from different cultural and linguistic backgrounds can be helped to maximize their full potential.
5. Identify and explain teaching models.

DISCUSSION AND STUDY ACTIVITIES

Discussion and study activities for Step Six include, but are not limited to the following:
1. Make clear and simple rules with your students' help.
2. Treat each student as the most valuable person in your classroom.
3. Do not play the "blame" game (i.e., blaming everyone but yourself).
4. Allow students to have some space and control in the learning environment.
5. Teach information that relates to your students.
6. Be flexible and sensitive, but do not patronize your audience.
7. Greet each person as he/she enters your classroom.
8. Use collaborative and consultative team approach for learning and teaching.
9. Ask and answer questions in nonthreatening manners in your class or program.
10. Demonstrate knowledge about interests, strengths, and weaknesses brought by each person to the learning environment.

Name: Date:

EXAMINATION
Following are examination questions based on objectives and pertinent ideas of Step
Six of *The Eight-Step Multicultural Approach*:

1.   You have an African American, a Native American, an Asian American, a
      Hispanic American, and an Anglo American in your classroom. Briefly
      describe how you can maximize their learning potential.

2.   **Analyze the concept of individual differences. Relate your answer to teaching in a multicultural learning environment.**

3. Choose *one* teaching theory or model and explain how this model relates to multicultural education.

4.   **Evaluate why a good teacher should be a good student.**

5.   **In two paragraphs, summarize why teachers should teach with divergent techniques.**

STEP SEVEN

MAKE THE RIGHT CHOICES

Step Seven, Make the Right Choices, suggests that the choices we make are based on our knowledge or lack of knowledge of who we are. To a large extent, the choices we make affect the decisions we make, and vice versa (Obiakor, 1994). There is nothing more rewarding than having some knowledge and having the ability to use that knowledge. By so doing, we become the architects of our own future. The critical question is, Do we understand why we are doing what we are doing? The answer to this question must always be a "Yes." If not, we are in the wrong profession. Our success in our profession depends on our ability to take charge of our lives; and our failure depends on our inability to take charge (Goleman, 1995). The latter results in the "blame game" (Obiakor, 1998).

Step Seven contains many teaching models that will help general and special educators to make the right choices. The first model, the *United States Interdependency Model* (USIM) demonstrates the powerful nature of the United States in the world scene. While the United States depends on other countries for natural resources, other countries depend on it for technical and financial supports. The second model, the *Multiethnic Model* (MM) highlights the ethnic strengths of immigrants and original settlers of the United States. The third model, the *Inclusive Model* (IM) indicates how an inclusive classroom (IC) is the result of a multicultural classroom (MC), cooperative classroom (CC), and collaboration (C), partnership (P), and consultation (C). The fourth model, the *Teach-Reteach Modification Model* (TRMM) reiterates the cyclical relationship between teaching and testing. The fifth model, the *Opportunity and Choice Model* (OCM) highlights the advantages of providing opportunities and choices for all students, especially multicultural learners. The sixth model, the *Retention Model* (RM) explains that multicultural learners must not only be accepted and acclimatized, they must also be made responsible and productive. It is not enough to tolerate people because of external pressures (e.g., federal laws). This results in negative feelings. We must include multicultural learners the same way we include White learners to eradicate invisibility. As professionals, we must take charge and make the right choices. We cannot continue to be victims of our circumstances. Our future certainly depends on our ability to be innovative on how we solve existing societal problems (see Obiakor, 1994, 1998).

LEARNING-TEACHING OBJECTIVES

After reading Step Seven, the learner will be able to:
1. Identify teaching models.
2. Evaluate implications of teaching models on the education of multicultural learners.
3. Describe the relationship between the choice he/she makes and the decision he/she makes.
4. Explain "success" as it relates to his/her chosen profession.
5. Evaluate a teaching model that best represents his/her teaching philosophy.

DISCUSSION AND STUDY ACTIVITIES

Discussion and study activities for Step Seven include, but are not limited to the following:

1. Choose to educate yourself on things that you do not know (e.g., the role of the news media).
2. Avoid assumptions about race, gender, culture, socio-economic status, and disability.
3. Integrate a wide variety of cultures into your teaching or programming to reflect the world-view.
4. Develop creative ideas (e.g., play, art, poetry, and music) that foster community interactions.
5. Value and celebrate differences that your students bring to class.
6. Create an atmosphere that empowers parents, staff, and administration.
7. Integrate individuals in projects and assignments.
8. Create bridges that connect different theoretical and teaching models.
9. Allow students or program participants to create models.
10. View the classroom as a machine which when fine-tuned can do wonderful things.

EXAMINATION

Following are examination questions based on objectives and pertinent ideas of Step Seven of *The Eight-Step Multicultural Approach*:

1.   Based on your personal experiences, briefly describe *two* choices that you have made and how these choices have helped you to make great decisions.

2. **Choose a teaching model and explain how this model best represents your teaching philosophy.**

3. Briefly examine how you can make the right choices in your chosen profession.

4.   Compare and contrast two teaching models presented in Step Seven.

5. "Our success in our profession depends on our ability to take charge of our lives; and our failure depends on our inability to take charge." Evaluate this statements using the knowledge that you have gained.

STEP EIGHT

CONTINUE TO LEARN

Step Eight, Continue to Learn, simply urges us to continue learning in this age of change. We cannot afford to close our minds to the "novel" (Obiakor, 1994). We stop learning when we are dead — life is learning, and learning is life. A good teacher must be a good learner — education is not education unless we can experience it or experiment on it. The more we learn, the less we make unwarranted presumptions about individuals, groups, races, religions, genders, skin colors, and nations. These presumptions frequently lead to prejudicial judgments, biased expectations, racist generalizations, and illusory conclusions (Obiakor, 1994; Grossman, 1998a, 1998b).

The life we live is useless unless we continue to learn. General and special educators must continue to learn how students who talk, look, behave, and learn differently are identified, assessed, and instructed. Traditional ways of doing things have not been very fruitful. Many multicultural learners continue to be misidentified, misassessed, miscategorized, misplaced, and misinstructed (see Grossman, 1998a, 1998b). To eliminate these phenomena, general and special educators must learn to modify and adapt their techniques to meet the specific needs of these students — their needs can no longer be swept under the rug. Teacher educators and school districts must begin to respond to accreditation demands of multicultural education. New courses must be offered to reflect the changing times (Obiakor, 1997). For instance, there must be courses on Multicultural Psychology and Special Education, Collaboration/Consultation, Self-Concept Development in Children and Youth, and Crisis Intervention (Obiakor, Mehring, & Schwenn, 1997). These courses will address multidimensional problems challenging all learners, especially those who come from different racial, cultural, linguistic and socio-economic backgrounds. We must understand current trends (e.g., Information Highways) and their implications to our sacred existence as a multicultural nation. In addition, we must understand the *Comprehensive Support Model* (CSM) (i.e., the relationship between the "self," the family, the school, and the community). We must continue to learn that no change will come to fruition unless we collaborate and consult with each other. Families, schools, and communities must work together if we are to make a difference (Dettmer, Dyck, & Thurston, 1996). The future seems bright; however, we cannot maximize the fullest potential of this bright future if we do not continue to learn new ways to solve problems (Utley & Obiakor, 1997).

LEARNING-TEACHING OBJECTIVES

After reading Step Eight, the learner will be able to:
1. Explain current problems facing general and special education.
2. Examine future challenges facing multicultural learners.
3. Explain why general and special educators must continue to learn.
4. Evaluate the relationship between families, schools, and communities.
5. Identify courses that will assist educators to respond to the changing times.

DISCUSSION AND STUDY ACTIVITIES

Discussion and study activities for Step Eight include, but are not limited to the following:

1. Demonstrate awareness of changes that are occurring in your community, society, nation, and world.
2. Learn the true history of various cultures and teach them to your class/group.
3. Teach from divergent perspectives; do not focus on the Eurocentric viewpoint alone.
4. Join multicultural groups to learn from others.
5. Talk seriously with people who look, learn, behave, and speak differently.
6. Value an outlook on life which places each daily experience in the realm of an important learning opportunity.
7. Create opportunities for authentic problem-solving (e.g., traveling to a new location, living with someone of a different culture, or joining a fraternity/sorority of a different race).
8. Learn new information about assessment and instruction.
9. Use collaborative examples to show your students that learning never ends.
10. Take a course that deals with challenging issues in today's changing world.

Name: **Date:**

EXAMINATION

Following are examination questions based on objectives and pertinent ideas of Step Eight of *The Eight-Step Multicultural Approach*:

1.   Briefly explain why you should continue to learn.

2. "The more we learn, the less we make unwarranted presumptions about individuals, groups, races, religions, genders, skin colors, and nations." Evaluate this statement using examples discussed in this course.

3.   Identify *two* traditional methods of working with multicultural learners. Briefly explain why these methods have been fruitless.

4. Examine future challenges that face multicultural learners in general and special education.

5.   Describe the relationship between families, schools, and communities. In your answer, explain the benefits of such a relationship.

REFERENCES

Baca, L. M., & Cervantes, H. P. (1991). *Bilingual special education* (ERIC Digest # E496). Reston, VA: The ERIC Clearinghouse on Handicapped and Gifted Education, Council for Exceptional Children.

Banks, J. A. (1999). *An introduction to multicultural education* (2nd ed.). Boston, MA: Allyn and Bacon.

Dettmer, P., Dyck, M., & Thurston, L. P. (1996). *Consultation, collaboration, and teamwork for students with special needs.* Boston, MA: Allyn and Bacon.

Ford, B. A., Obiakor, F. E., & Patton, J. M. (1995). *Effective education of African American exceptional learners: New perspectives.* Austin, TX: Pro-Ed.

Gardner, H. (1993). *Multiple intelligences: The theory in practice.* New York: Basic Books.

Goleman, D. (1995). *Emotional intelligence: Why it can matter more than IQ.* New York: Bantam Books.

Gollnick, D. M., & Chinn, P. C. (1998). *Multicultural education in a pluralistic society* (5th ed.). Upper Saddle River, NJ: Prentice-Hall.

Gould, S.J. (1981). *The mismeasure of man.* New York: Norton.

Grossman, H. (1998a). *Achieving educational equality: Assuring all students an equal opportunity in school.* Springfield, IL: Charles C. Thomas.

Grossman, H. (1998b). *Ending discrimination in special education.* Springfield, IL: Charles C. Thomas.

Hilliard, A. S. (1995). Culture, assessment, and valid teaching for the African American student. In B. A. Ford, F. E. Obiakor, & J. M. Patton (Eds.), *Effective education of African American exceptional learners: New perspectives* (pp. ix-xvi). Austin, TX: Pro-Ed.

Obiakor, F. E. (1994). *The eight-step multicultural appoach: Learning and teaching with a smile.* Dubuque, IA: Kendall/Hunt.

Obiakor, F. E. (1997, Spring). Shifting paradigms: Responding to cultural diversity in teacher preparation programs. *DDEL News, 7,* 6.

Obiakor, F. E. (1998, August 24). Make your own destiny. *Emporia State University Bulletin, 98,* p. 17.

Obiakor, F. E., & Algozzine, B. (1994, Fall). Self-concept of young children with special needs: Perspectives for school and clinic. *Canadian Journal of School Psychology, 10,* 123-30.

Obiakor, F. E., & Algozzine, B. (1995). *Managing problem behaviors: Perspectives for general and special educators.* Dubuque, IA: Kendall/Hunt.

Obiakor, F. E., Algozzine, B., & Campbell-Whatley, G. (1997). Self-concept: Intervention and assessment. *Australian Journal of Learning Disabilities, 2,* 17-22.

Obiakor, F. E., Campbell-Whatley, G., Schwenn, J. O., & Dooley, E. (1998). Emotional first-aids for exceptional learners. In A. F. Rotatori, J. O. Schwenn, & S. Burkhardt (Eds.), *Advances in special education: Issues, practices and concerns in special education* (Vol. 11, pp. 171-185). Greenwich, CT: JAI Press.

Obiakor, F. E., Mehring, T. A., & Schwenn, J. O. (1997). *Disruption, disaster, and death: Helping students deal with crises.* Reston, VA: The Council for Exceptional Children.

Obiakor, F. E., & Schwenn, J. O. (1995). Enhancing self-concepts of culturally diverse students: The role of the counselor. In A. F. Rotatori, J. O. Schwenn, & F. W. Litton (Eds.), *Advances in special education: Counseling special populations* (Vol. 10, pp. 37-57). Greenwich, CT: JAI Press.

Obiakor, F. E., & Stile, S. W. (1994). *Self-concepts of exceptional learners: Current perspectives for educators* (rev. printing). Dubuque, IA: Kendall/Hunt.

Obiakor, F.E., & Utley, C.A. (1997). Rethinking preservice preparation for teachers in the learning disabilities field: Workable multicultural strategies. *Learning Disabilities Research & Practice, 12*, 100-106.

Pederson, P. B. (1991, September/October). Multiculturalism as a generic approach to counseling. *The Journal of Counseling and Development, 70*, 6-12.

Utley, C. A., & Obiakor, F. E. (1997). *Addressing diversity in special education research* (ERIC/OSEP Digest #E561). Reston, VA: The ERIC Clearinghouse on Disabilities and Gifted Education, Council for Exceptional Children.

Winzer, M. A., & Mazurek, K. (1998). *Special education in multicultural contexts*. Upper Saddle River, NJ: Prentice-Hall.

Festus E. Obiakor, Ph.D., is Professor of Psychology and Special Education and Coordinator, Graduate Mental Retardation Program, Supervisor/Coordinator of Special Education Program, and Director of Special Education Program, Emporia State University, Emporia, Kansas. He is a national leader and consultant in the field of special education. In addition, he is on the editorial board of many scholarly publications, including *Exceptional Children* and *Multiple Voices* - he currently serves as Associate Editor of both journals. He is the author of more than 100 publications, including books, chapters, articles, commentaries, and poetry. His areas of interest include self-concept development, multicultural psychology and special education, crisis intervention/ management, collaboration/consultation, educational reform/program evaluation, and comparative/ international special education.